I0402522

ANALYZING REAL ESTATE INVESTING

INVESTING

*FUNDAMENTALS OF FINDING
INCOME PROPERTIES FOR A
PROFITABLE INVESTMENT*

OSWALD TOWNSEND

ANALYZING REAL ESTATE INVESTING

Copyright© 2019 by Aculeatus Limited.
All Rights Reserved.

No part of this book may be reproduced in any form or by any electronic or mechanical means including information storage and retrieval systems, without permission in writing from the author. The only exception is by a reviewer, who may quote short excerpts in a review.

Cover designed by pro_ebookcovers, CA, USA

OSWALD TOWNSEND
Visit amazon.com/author/oswaldtownsend

Printed in the United States of America
First Printing: October 2019
ISBN-13: 9781696566063
Imprint: Independently published

For all endangered species facing mass extinction

CONTENTS

A man's character is his fate.

Heraclicus

1 INTRODUCTION

Throughout history, real estate has proven an accomplishable and feasible investment vehicle. It seems that those that control the real estate end up with wealth. The great civilizations of the Egyptians, Greeks, Persians, and Mayans, as well as the mighty Roman, Ottoman, Chinese and British empires, all, had massive real estate holdings as part of their power structure. At the beginning of the twentieth century, the British were reported to own one-fourth of the world's landmass. Well, as we know, in those days obtaining and possessing the land and real estate was not exclusively based on purchasing it from their owners. As Alfred Krupp, the richest industrialist in Europe during the late 19th Century, once said, "More money has been made in real estate than in all industrial investments combined."

Today, investing in real estate requires much more finesse, good timing, and sophisticated strategies. This book aims to provide the readers and the real estate investors with applicable answers for addressing all of these issues.

2 REAL ESTATE INVESTING: WHAT, WHY AND HOW?

A t present day, investors hold several pieces of real estate. They own these pieces of land so that they benefit from lease revenue generation, gains by price appreciation, and also for residential purposes. This revenue which is utilized by them to create lease income, is entitled as real estate investment. The levy implications applied to real estate investment differ from the ones applied to residential real estate. Following the definition as mentioned above of real estate, a few examples include residential complexes and rental units which are employed for yielding rental revenue from occupants and not for residential purposes. As the worth of each estate appreciates over a while, investors also look forward to acquiring capital gains.

Categorization of Real Estate Investment

Categorization of real estate will help you gather a better understanding of the whole picture. If you are interested in owning a real estate, it will facilitate you in opting for the best alternative. Here is the list:

Residential:

Properties such as homes, residential complexes, etc. are the residential locations for which a family pays lease amount to the proprietor for the duration of their stay. Such lease revenue-generating holdings are termed as residential estates or structure. To stay in these residential pieces, the lessee and the owner sign a lease agreement. This contract also comprises the information regarding the duration of the tenant's stay.

Commercial:

If a person is willing to invest in the commercial estate, then he/she should construct a building with the savings they possess. Then that individual can then rent out those buildings to minor office branches and high-rise buildings to generate lease-based revenue. At present day, holding multi-annual leases has become an ordinary thing. These multi-year lease systems possess an edge as well as a drawback. The edge of multi-annual lease systems is that they ensure a stable inflow and outflow of cash. That stability proves to be of great help when there is a drop in the lease rates. But the drawback of such systems is that, if the lease rates considerably rise in the market, it may be impossible to run the estate as your deal is sealed with the office lessees in the former contract.

Industrial:

Industrial storehouses, distribution hubs, storage units, car washing stations, and diverse ad-hoc real estate that yield turnover from consumers underlie in the category of the industrial real estate. Industrial estate investments usually hold a considerable fee amount and service cash flows. Coin-based vacuum cleaners at a car wash station make a great example for the service cash flow system, which also proves to be a great way of raising the ROI of the proprietor.

Retail:

In case of retail estates, a few proprietors acquire a portion of the turnover created by the tenant besides the actual lease amount. This sum is provided to the holder by the lessee for ensuring the first-class maintenance of the premises. Some pieces of the estate that underlie in the category of retail properties include shopping complexes, open-air shopping complexes, and other retail display cases.

Mixed-Use:

Estates that are found merged in a singular structure and which comprises of the pieces as mentioned earlier of estates all under one roof are termed as mixed-use possessions.

How to Invest in Real Estate?

One of the most sought after and the oldest asset classes in the industry is real estate, and no wonder every new investor wants to get a taste of the market that promises good growth and great returns. But before entering the lucrative market, it is important to know the different types of investments one can make in real estate.

Just like every other investment people opt for, real estate also renders diverse choices. And just like every mode of investment that promises great returns, real estate also comes with its own set of advantages and disadvantages. Hence it becomes crucial for investors to acquire a deep understanding of lending traditions, cash flow cycles, and market standards before they start investing. While it is important to understand the diverse real estate market and all the above factors, it is also important to specialize in a specific niche. And as people start exploring and acquiring deep insights about a specific niche, it takes them no time to make a fortune.

Therefore, it becomes important to pick a niche and to spend a significant amount of efforts, resources, and time to understand its ins and outs to achieve financial independence and to generate a passive income effectively. There are various ways to make the most out of the real estate investment, and investors can choose from diverse paths to make profitable investments. An investor can either opt for an investment group for real estate which acquires properties by pooling funds, or the property holder can hire managers to ensure the proper maintenance and collection of rent for a property. Real estate also allows investors to generate good returns by letting him/her serve on funding or lending side of the complete project. This method involves giving loans for good interest rates or acquiring the ownership of the piece of that particular real estate if there is a possibility of great resale value.

Real estate investors can also opt for a property that's underdeveloped or is in poor condition. The benefit of investing in such a property is that it enables the investors to renovate the property and make it suitable as well as attractive for the residents, which promises great long terms returns. The location of the property also plays an important role when it comes to real estate investment. In today's fast-paced lives, people generally look for a property in the middle of the city. Hence investing in real estate which is surrounded by attractions, highway extensions, malls, shops, and good infrastructure makes a piece of property extremely desirable and also promises good returns on sale as well as long term higher rent due to high demand.

Why to Invest in Real Estate?

Real estate investment can offer an individual with several edges which other investment alternatives might fail to provide. It comprises of advantages like potentially higher yields, immutability, inflation hedging, and multifariousness. Here are a few root causes to take into account for investing in real estate.

Competitive Risk-Adjusted Returns:

According to a report published by the National Council of Real Estate Investment Fiduciaries (NCREIF) on July 2018, the private market, commercial real estate returned an average proportion of 9.85 percent in the recent five years. This plausible execution was accomplished, jointly with low instability about equities and bonds, for intensely competitive risk-adjusted returns.

Critics debate about the fact that low instable peculiarity of real estate is the outcome of sporadic real estate transactions and estate values which are usually fixed by third-party evaluations. These evaluations tend to linger the market behind. The sporadic transactions and evaluations result in the smoothening of returns, as announced possession values underrate market values in boon period and overrate market values in recession.

While it is fair to say that historical evaluations of real estate instability should be adjusted in an upstream manner, real-time marketplaces are exposed to abrupt unanticipated shocks. The "Flash Crash" of May 2010 is a good example of demonstrating unanticipated shocks. Stable prices of real estate are appealing in an environment where market instability is an issue, and the dynamics of algorithmic trading are cloudy.

High Tangible Asset Value:

An investment in real estate is supported by a high proportion of brick and mortar, unlike stocks and bonds. This field of investment facilitates in minimizing the principal-agent conflict or the degree to which the curiosity of the investor is reliant on the honesty and know-how of managers and debtors. Even real estate investment trusts (REITs), which are listed real estate securities, usually possess regulations that make it obligatory to pay out a minimal proportion of proceeds as dividends.

Attractive and Steady Income Return:

An essential feature of real estate investment is the considerable percentage of entire return accruing from lease income in the long run. Real estate return facilitates minimizing instability when it is derived from income flows. As investments that depend more on income return tend to be less unstable, compared to those that depend more on capital value return. Real estate is also appealing in comparison to conventional sources of revenue return.

Portfolio Diversification:

Diversification potential is another edge of investing in real estate. Real estate has a low, and in some cases, unfavorable, correspondence with other significant categories of assets. This fact implies that the accumulation of real estate to a portfolio of miscellaneous assets can reduce portfolio instability and can offer an increased return per unit of risk.

Inflation Hedging:

Positive correlation amidst GDP growth and the demand for real estate are the components that facilitate the emergence of the inflation hedging ability of real estate. The demand for real estate impels rents to heighten and this, in turn, converts into increased capital values, as nations develop and grow. Therefore, real estate tends to preserve the spending power of capital by transiting some of the inflationary spirals on to lessees and by including a couple of the inflationary spiral in terms of capital appreciation.

The Drawback: Insufficiency of Liquidity:

The illiquidity or the relative trouble of transforming an asset into cash and cash into an asset is the primary disadvantage of investing in real estate. A real estate transaction might take months to close, whereas a stock or bond transaction can be accomplished in seconds. Even with the assistance acquired from a real estate agent, merely discovering the right counterparty can be the work of a couple of weeks.

3 RECOGNIZING BEST REAL ESTATE OPPORTUNITIES

Oe of the key benefits of investing in real estate is the benefit of infinite choices. No matter what your budget is, real estate always has something to offer as per your requirements. But since there are endless choices, the task of investing can put you into some serious dilemma. Hence an investor needs to recognize the trends and opportunities in real estate that will help generate maximum profits.

While there are many factors which might make an investment opportunity seem good, there are three factors which will create some of the best investment opportunities.

The three factors are:

(1) Cash-on-cash return: Cash-on-cash-return is the amount of cash earned on the amount of cash invested in a property. The goal of an investor must be to increase the difference between the two that is, to increase the cash-on-cash return. If a real estate has positive cash flow and promises great cash-on-cash return, it can be one of the best investment opportunities. Investors can easily calculate the value of cash-on-cash return with the help of an investment calculator on any specific property.

(2) Low-risk or safe investments: In the volatile market, one can never be sure about the returns since the prices shift unpredictably. Hence if someone manages to get their hands on a property that imposes low-risk, it could be one of the safest and best real estate investments. This usually involves a property on which you'll have complete ownership and which has a simple and clear cash flow. Before investing, make sure you carry out complete property analysis to ensure that you are opting for a low-risk and safe investment option for real estate.

(3) Minimum property management and time: One of the best ways to invest in real estate is to invest in a property which can be put on rent quickly and requires minimum management. Hence investing in rentable properties not only gives you good returns for the long term but also helps in making property management a painless task

How to Recognize Great Real Estate Opportunities?

One of the means that can yield you a good and rapid ROI is by seeking a great real estate opportunity. Every estate holder would want the best bid while trading their property. While the cost of the possession also counts, your capability to distinguish if the investment is worthy is very crucial, and this requires a very watchful eye.

Here are some of the means that you can utilize to understand good real estate opportunities that are worth your money.

Follow the Golden Rule:

The common golden rule or the 1% rule in real estate stipulates that the revenue of the possession that you desire to invest in should lease for at least 1% of the selling price. This rule will facilitate in generating some good cash flow.

The rule also implies you have to be aware of how many leases the occupants are paying, or the ongoing market lease rate for identical estates in the area so that you can possess the knowledge about the return which you will acquire from the property.

Be aware of the Class of the Property:

Properties are graded underneath diverse categories; class A, B, and C. Class A category possess the topmost quality in the real estate market, as it is primarily new and is traded at higher rates. Class B is former, but well-tended holdings and class C are a little more former than class B, and they also need fixes and refurbishment. The superior most investment is either class B or C, as they will not restrict you on the sort of occupants that you can possess. Such possessions require a little refinishing here and there; you will surely have a flow of lessees which, in turn, imply timely pay.

Know Your Potential Tenants:

The potential lessees of the estate that you wish to invest in will facilitate you in identifying whether you are making a good investment or not.

Recognize the Market and Submarkets:

Areas vulnerable to employment opportunities, development, and population are key factors that help in determining the righteous location for your estate. Scrutinize the areas where new shopping complexes, new institutions, new interconnecting roads, and highways. Always keep in mind factors such as the occupants and the reselling value. These factors imply possessions close to urban areas, eateries, public transit, and shopping complexes. These real estates are feasible to invest in than holdings located in remote and lavish localities. Furthermore, it is more relatable to business rather than your preference alternatives. To make a righteous investment, you have to think about profit.

Foreclosed Properties Are Great Real Estate Properties:

Purchasing a foreclosed estate implies that you are gaining from someone else's loss. They can prove to be good investments. Financers and banks managing foreclosed properties are never curious about managing or possessing them. Financial establishments take a greater interest in getting their cashback. This behavior implies that such holdings are a great trade because they can liquidate quickly.

Evaluate the Selling Price against the County Appraisal Value

If you desire to know the current worth of your estate, then visit the county appraisal district website and enter the address of your possession and find out its value under the county's assessment. You can be sure about making a good profit from your estate when the purchase price is way beneath the county appraisal value. This is because the county appraisal value fixes the fair market value in addition to some proportion over their assessment depending on the territory.

Compute the Cap Rate

The capitalization rate is computed by splitting your yearly net revenue minus any expenditure by the cost of the estate you wish to purchase. If the holding is yielding you a cap rate of 10%, then it is a feasible investment opportunity.

Your capability to anticipate opportunities and proceeds where others see difficulties is one of the things that will facilitate you in making good investments when considering investment in real estate.

4 BEST TIME AND WAYS TO ENTER REAL ESTATE MARKETS

Just like every other mode of investment, real estate is also an investment that heavily relies on timing. There are times when investing in real estate can be your smartest move and can help you generate huge profits, and there are times when your whole investment can bring you huge losses. Hence it is important to be mindful of the following time-sensitive factors which influence the real estate greatly. Also, evaluating these factors will help you predict the market and decide the best time to invest.

Incredibly low-interest rates:

When a property has low-interest rates, it automatically implies low payments every month. The relationship between the two is highly beneficial for investors who look forward to reaping maximum returns. Though the interest rates have been increasing slowly, the most recent analysis revealed few facts about the shaky market, one of which implied that the traders are now advocating a chance of less than 8% increase in rate throughout this year.

Banks to the rescue:

The real estate market witnessed its crash in the years 2007 and 2008. Because of this, many banks created strict policies which made it incredibly difficult for thousands of people to obtain a mortgage. However, in past years, banks have become a bit flexible in terms of their policies and have started lending once again. If an investor has maintained his credit over the years and has a decent job or a successful business, obtaining a loan on fixed rate should be easy.

Reasonable prices of foreclosures:
Thought the prices in real estate had increased significantly, one can still find a decent deal at low costs. And one of the best ways to find these low-cost deals is to explore the bank foreclosures.

As per the statistics provided by RealtyTrac, a real estate information company and an online marketplace for foreclosed and defaulted properties in the United States, 100,000 foreclosed properties were filed on May 2016 alone, and they were easily available at low prices.

Harnessing the power of technology for investing:
Gone are the times when buying a property used to be a daunting task. Hours of driving, walking, exploring, talking, and flipping thousands of pages of the contact books had not only made people dread the task but also had made the process extremely complex. But today, people can easily harness the power of technology to browse thousands of properties on their fingertips. One can make use of property listing websites, sign up to receive property listings directly on their mail, order cleaning and maintenance services online, take virtual tours via Google street view, set up online modes for payment collection from tenants, etc. There is no doubt that technology has revolutionized the experience of buying property completely.

The abundance of knowledge:
There was a time when the real estate "gurus" would charge huge fees from people to hand them the recipe of the secret sauce. While some of these gurus can be easily spotted even today, the internet has ended most of their careers. The internet provides millions of blog posts, free seminars, podcasts, forums, eBook, and many more resources, which help the investors to not only connect but also make wise decisions.

The unstable job:

There was a time when people would spend their whole lives in one single cubicle. But the golden days are over. Today, job security has become a myth, and big giants in the industry do not hesitate to let go of thousands of employees. Only those with skills are thriving in the industry and hence investing in real estate is one path that anyone can take to achieve financial independence.

Start today before it's too late:

Just like a tree takes years to grow and produce sweet and juicy fruits, your investment will also take years to mature and generate profits. Investing today might not get you instant returns, but years from now, most people will look back and wonder what stopped them from investing. Today is the best day to plan and invest, and if you keep on waiting, you might miss out on some of the greatest opportunities.

How to Enter Even the Most Competitive Markets?

Investing in real estate has erupted in the last few years. One of the majorly common grievances heard from new investors is that their market is very competitive.

While this might be the case, but there are means to battle it. Entering a highly-competitive market only implies that there are plenty of deals to go around. Here are a bunch of strategies and notions that can facilitate you in entering even the most competitive markets.

Have Knowledge of Your Competition:

It is crucial to know your competition if you are planning to get into the real estate market. Have a look at the sorts of trading that are thanking place in that particular market. No matter what the nook is, you wouldn't want to get engulfed in it. The reason behind you becoming interested in investing might have been foreclosure investing, but you are required to generate your niche.

Most prosperous enterprises either outshine at their area of work or they discover an alternative means to create a volume of business, irrespective of the industry. There exists not much of a difference in the case of real estate as well. If there are ten investors all after the same estate, it is more sensible to observe the areas that possess little competitive.

If your decision of existing in a certain market is firm, then you need to know why certain investors are prosperous. This information could imply searching for diverse property kinds or examining diverse markets. By examining your competition, you can get an excellent idea of how and where to you will be planning to take your business. Inspect where the prosperous investors acquire their contracts from and the quality of the end product.

Value Added Networking:
Entering a market usually requires a persistent squad around you. To establish your crew, you need to network. There exists a misapprehension that all networking is the same. Meeting new individuals and assembling visiting cards is nice, but that may not be enough to assist you in expanding your business.

Networking yourself requires you put yourself in someone's situation. Question yourself about the rationale you are providing to someone to collaborate/work with you by emphasizing on what value you include in the relationship for building a more powerful networking foundation. A broker may possess five other investors towards whom he can turn to with a foreclosure. 'How your way of functioning is different from others' should be included in your thought process while addressing every new individual. If you possess something that is beneficial for them or makes their job a whole lot easier, then they will surely remember you.

Focused Marketing:
The way you promote your business is essential when you are planning on entering into an area of work or entering a market. There exists an instinct to opt

for any marketing and operate with it. But caution, that might be a formula for disaster.

Give a thought on the number of letters which are being posted to native landlords in foreclosure. Your letter would be more likely to be overlooked unless it genuinely sticks out. One of the amazing things about investing in real estate is that you can operate your business in the manner you prefer. Your marketing is supposed to be unique and exclusive. Search patiently for deals and estates that you might wish to acquire. More deals will come to your path if you are good at marketing.

Think Big Picture:

In an impeccable world, you will be capable of discovering home run deals as early as you step into the estate business. A much more pragmatic scenario is that you will have to construct your path to reach that point.

Deals with a lesser rate of returns will arise in your path, but you will have to consider them as well, whether you prefer or not. Everyone is well aware that their time is worth their money, but starting with these small deals might assist you in getting going. Every deal is not just about making money; they are accompanied by the edge of several contacts too. There possibly could exist up to five potential contacts per deal.

After finishing a few smaller deals, you can get identified in the estate market, and big opportunities will also knock at your door. You can never tell if an individual involved in a deal might know someone that could prove to be a perfect match for your business. On the way of constructing your property empire, there might be several sacrifices that you will have to make.

5 AVOIDING REAL ESTATE BUBBLES

The real estate bubble is known as the housing bubble, and this takes place due to a rapid increase in the price of the houses. The rapid hike in the prices takes place due to low supply, high demand, and emotional buying. The lucrative market then also attracts investors who want to generate quick profits, which contributes to increasing demand. For all the chaos, the term bubble is used as doesn't matter how lucrative the market seems, the bubble bursts at some point.

A deeper look at the real estate bubble:

In the year 2006, the prices of housing suddenly increased, and by the end, the prices started decreasing. In the year 2017, the real estate bubble finally witnessed its doom. The bubble finally burst, and everyone who had paid the extra price for their dream homes realized the blunder they had made and panicked. It didn't take much time for everyone to realize that they had made a bad investment as the returns were way less as compared to the price they had paid.

In the healthy market, when an investor makes an investment and acquires a property, he/she expects to witness an increase in the value slowly and steadily. Most investors are aware of the fact that building equity can take decades, and they make peace with this fact. While their investment grows, they still get to live in their own houses, and there are also tax deductions involved. Few of these investors also expect to make quick cash from their recent investments.

In case of investors who make decisions based on speculations, as the prices of the real estate start seeing faster hikes, they leap into the market to buy and sell quickly. The goal of these investors is to make quick money by selling the property to someone ready to make investments at a higher price. According to the research, real estate bubbles are a result of speculations, which are deeply rooted in the psychology of investors and buyers. The speculators buy multiple properties which make people throw away their financial senses and make bad investments.

How to avoid real estate bubbles?

Cost of the house as compared to your budget:

Everybody knows that money doesn't grow on trees. But how many people want to accept this fact? One of the most common mistakes that people make is that they believe they can manage finances and monthly payments, even when the house exceeds their budget. In the past, many banks and people completely ignored the traditional rules which were designed to keep things in place and make housing affordable for people, and this ignorance served as a cornerstone for all the mess in the economy.

One of the best ways to keep your finances in check is to ensure that your housing expense, which includes property taxes, principal, insurance and interest is not more than 25-28% of your complete monthly income. Spending half or more than half of the monthly income for keeping a roof over your head is a big no-no. Most of the people buy lavish houses by saying that they are a two-income household, but as one of them loses his/her job, the income reduces to half, which creates a panicky situation. Hence there are many advantages of keeping the housing expenses low. Not only it helps you save money for your next investment, but also helps you keep funds for any emergency.

A down payment is important:

During the latest real estate bubble, those who opted for the zero down payment loans suffered the most. People quickly wanted to acquire the assets in real estate, and banks quickly wanted to generate money. Result? Everyone got to learn the bitter lesson about real estate – that prices don't always go up, and the values of houses can also put the investors underwater.

While there are still some zero down payment loans available for people, it is important to make sure you pay the initial amount. The larger your down payment is, the less you'll need to finance, which also lowers your interest rates and monthly payments. Another benefit of paying the down payment is that it provides you with a financial cushion. Even if you manage to pay 20% down payment and you don't see the rise in the price, you'll still be in a good position. But if there is no down payment involved and the value of your property falls, you'll get stuck in a messy situation, and you'll lose a lot of money if you decide to sell in the future.

Buying homes wisely without rushing:

To make sure that you don't get stuck in the future real estate bubble, it's important to ensure that you have an appropriate reason to buy. Many people dream about acquiring their own home, but this dream is hard-wired in the system of many people from a young age. While it's fine to think about buying your casa, one must make sure that they are making conscious and wise decisions. Jumping to invest big sums of money just because you are fed up with paying rent, you are about to get married, or you are planning to start a family is a big no.

Before taking any decision, a little introspection is important. Asking yourself why you want to buy a home will reveal a lot about your thought process, emotions, and requirements. If you manage to uncover the facts which require you to buy a home, you can start looking for one that fits your budget and monthly income structure.

If your job requires you to move a lot from city to city and might also make you move to another city in the future, renting for two to three years might prove to be a better option instead of buying a house.

Last but not least, never misjudge or miscalculate all the hidden expenses that add up with home-ownership. Only the maintenance of a house can cost you hundreds of dollars per month and can easily burn a hole in your pocket. Hence to avoid the financial drain, it becomes important to calculate everything precisely and make wise decisions.

6 BEST TIME TO ENTER AND EXIT A PARTICULAR MARKET

To acquire the most beneficial deal, you need to have precise research of the major purchase you are about to make. Hence before confirming the purchase, it is vital to grab as much possible information on the real estate market. The amount that you would pay for a property can be hugely varied by selecting the appropriate time of buying, irrespective you are buying the property with an objective of investment or for your personal use. So, what would be the perfect time for buying a property?

Trace Pricing Trends:
It will bind you in a 15 to 30-year long debt if you go for a usual mortgage loan. For whatever purpose, if you are planning to sell your property, it would be a delaying task. Hence it is always important to be up with your research and make appropriate choices for real-estate purchase.

Timing plays a major role in real estate. The investment must be made during the time of the buyer's market. A buyer's market occurs when the number of sellers exceeds the number of buyers present in the market. However, tracing this type of market is difficult; no matter you are a pro-investor or a fresher. You need to decide the location where you want to make a purchase and also have to track the price trends persisting in the current scenario. The perfect time to buy the property is when the expected prices at a particular date are higher than the actual price for which the property is quoted at the same time. A property's span in the market helps you to determine its demand in the market. As long as the property stays in the market, its demand moves at a declining rate. In the case of high demand, the market experiences high pricing of the property.

Time of the year:

Purchasing a residential property during winters at a place with severe cold issues would be a bad choice. You might be stuck into a snowstorm or get frozen into the ice. This is the reason why home purchases during winters are never considered to be ideal. For the fact that winters are not ideal for moving in a home, the prices of residential properties would become low. Although, there could be a shortage in inventory as before showing up a property in the market, a lot of people like to refurbish and renovate it during winters.

Despite getting a worthful value, you must not hurry with your purchase decision. You must wait for fewer more properties that come into the market in the time of spring, as they could be comparatively better in terms of longevity, feasibility, and value. Probably it will cost you higher, but it would be the perfect purchase for you and your family.

Personal finances:

You need to be firm with your decision to buy out a property, before entering into the research and market exposure step. You need to be sure that best interest rates are offered to you and also you have to confirm that the rate of credits is maximum. Waiting until a perfect credit could help you save quite a lot of money. Also, you would require 20% of your savings ready as a deposit. You can save from private mortgage insurance by paying 20% as a deposit for your home; this will save your money in future terms as well. Well exploring all the available loan options is a good choice before selecting one.

You can save money by applying a hard money loan, an FHA loan, or multi-family loan rather than just sticking with a traditional mortgage loan option for your investment property. The route you choose must guide you to the maximum savings on interest rates for purchasing a real estate.

What should be the appropriate time to leave the real estate market?

When the Actual Prices are low:

In case, asset allocation says the portfolio's rebalancing is necessary, then possibly you won't be able to forecast the short-term returns and hence should not delay. The prices of the residential property won't hike if there are regular additions of new projects and rigid regulations continue. Here the inventories are considered to be in metros. An alternative investment can show a similar payoff to the investors in such a situation. Based on the underlying asset's size, the professionals of real estate can provide help to gain an outlook for investors.

One must keep its investment perspective durable, no matter the investment is made in a tangible asset like real estate or a monetary asset like mutual funds. The lowest period must be at least 10 to 15 years. The abnormal movement of price in the past leads the investors to anticipate unusual returns within short periods. Due to mental predictions of an asset, the investors do not let go of the asset, even if it is making a loss.

The classes of assets have their cycle, which goes ups and downs. Classification of the asset could be the wrong decision to drive maximum earning. A dedicated following of such assets would only land you into a high level of transaction costs, increased churn rate, and higher taxes. Its prediction cannot be made regularly or accurately.

Do Not Wait for Abnormal Benefits:

Despite the improvement in the Indian Real Estate lobby in terms of accountability and transparency, there are sub-optimal returns gained through asset classes in preceding 4 to 5 years. The days when money could be acquired easily by regularly flipping the property are gone. One needs to stay with the property in the market for a longer time to make average returns through it. The main purpose is to acquire returns that are similar to your objective; if the current situations meet it, you must not wait for uncertain gains. On a larger or macro scale, there is an improvement in the Indian market.

After the dust is settled, the property landscape would show its macro benefits. The market drive is now in the hands of new customers contradicting the investor who used to drive the real estate lobby earlier. Though, these new customers require reasonable and concise configurations. Hence the existence of demand drivers persists. No matter what is the present condition of the market, you must expose your property for exiting from the market if there is a need for alignment. The requirement of optimization of your asset mix would be required when you are re-aligning or re-balancing.

Invest Money in More Beneficial Options:

From investing strategy, the exit is sensible even if it's equal to one's cost price or 10 to 15% below of the one's cost price. Indulging a property for 5 to 6 years and then gaining 4 to 6% profit on it won't be as good as selling a property at lower 10% and then buying out something with 10 to 12% return value. The opportunity cost would be maximum, of the investor stays at hiked real estate exit price; it will also possibly land the investor into a situation where he has to bear a time correction for the longer term.

The benefits which investors gained by exiting asset years back and re-investing in financial assets are comparatively better liquidity, post-tax return, and flexibility. The case of exit in a real estate strengthens with RERA act, blocked real estate inventory in the market, attack on black money, and reduction in the tax advantages for a second home. These actions have affected the purchases in real estate, especially for investment purposes, for those who have 60% worth of real estate properties.

The investor will be able to have tax shelters if it has a record of holding an asset for more than two years. These tax shelters will be in the form of indexed loss for the long term in a case where the person adds indexation while filing an IT return.

Stick with Your Realty Investment:

In the current scenario, the selling of inventory is becoming a major task for developers. To have a favorable position of cash flow, the developers are forced to adjust their pricing below to their selling rate. Also, due to RERA deadlines, developers have to keep up with their deadlines and hence have to sell their stocks in pressure. For the last one year, the launches are getting low, though the increase in supply still stays. Though, the consumption of this increasing inventory may get fulfilled by 2020-21.

On the contrary, the leasing practices are showing better in the demand of the commercial real-estate sector. There is a positive relationship between the demand of commercial real estate and residential real estate, and if considered the present situations, the increasing interest in the commercial sector would also positively increase the demand of residential real estate though one has to wait until it happens.

As low sales are persisting in the current residential sector, the developers are high with discounts countering the inventory pressure. And for the owners of residential properties, they would be waiting for the equilibrium status of demand and supply in the market. You must wait until you see hope to the maximum extent.

7 CURRENT GLOBAL HOTSPOTS

Some of the top markets that make it to the list of world's best residential markets have witnessed a strong rise in investments in the past few decades. The market is still being dominated by the forerunners of real estate, namely, New York, London, and Miami. These cities sit on the top of the lists of investors and still are the first choice for many property buyers. But let's be real. Not everyone can buy property in these three cities. So, the question arises, in what other cities can people invest in and which cities can generate maximum returns on the investment? The Global Residential Forecast by the global real estate consultants Knight Frank for the year 2018 had clearly outlined the current scenario for the key purchasers and also examined the cities around the globe. So as per those reports, here are some cities which have proven to be the most promising hot spots for real state.

Berlin:

The market of Berlin sees new horizons in economic growth. The low priced and high-grade units of real estate are the main reasons behind the explosive economic growth. Equipped with the economy which is considered one of the best in the whole country, Berlin not only has caught the eyes of the investors because of its real estate but also has managed to make it to the list because of the low cost of living.

Paris:

Even though Paris faced its fair share of struggles with seeing the price hike in recent years, things have finally started to look good. The change is arriving slowly to the real estate market of the Paris, and the city is back on the list of the high-end global investors who are from Europe, the USA, and the Middle East.

The French capital is displaying all the signs like increase in interest, which signals towards healthy and steady price growth that can go up to 9%. The major reason behind this improvement is the shift of Eurozone's economic outlook. The recent cancellation of the rent caps across the city is also one of the main reasons why Paris has made it to the list.

Dubai:

Dubai sees a new rise in the employment rates, which has further contributed to the rise in demand for the properties. In the year 2018, Dubai displayed a humble growth in the economy, and today, the government is investing large sums of money in the infrastructure to prepare for the Expo 2020.

8 PROMISING FUTURE HOT SPOTS

O ne of the smartest moves an investor can make is to invest in one of the hot spots that have recently emerged. Not only these hot spots require low investment but also promise high returns in the future. But before investing, it is important to recognize the risks and the scope of development in the areas where you are planning to invest. These risks can involve delays by developers, delayed completion, etc. and these factors can easily take a toll on the resale value.

So, how can an investor who is planning to invest in the hotspots identify the pitfalls and make a wise decision? Well, there are few factors which can ensure a good investment.

Population growth:

Though the localities in these hotspots are developing and contain a small population, over time, these areas will become densely populated as more and more people will be investing and moving here. When people start to move to a specific locality, it becomes a key factor which helps investors identify the hotspots.

Infrastructure projects:

Another sign of an emerging hotspot is under construction infrastructure, which not only helps boost development in the future but also facilitates connectivity, creates more employment opportunities, and brings more amenities to a locality. Conducting thorough research about the upcoming projects and carrying out an effective property analysis will inform an investor about the timeline of these projects.

Price movement:

Carrying out a study to predict the past movements of property prices not only helps an investor predict future trends but also helps in making a wise decision. Even if the rise in the price is slow and steady, it can help you acquire a rough estimate of the moment of prices in the coming years.

High-growth area:

The best thing about high growth areas is suburbs also surround them. An investor can easily move a few kilometers away towards the suburbs to find real estate at affordable prices. When an investor opts for a property that is available in low price in the suburbs, these properties see a significant price hike in a span of three to four years.

The supply and demand ratio:

Before jumping to invest, it is important to know the ratio of demand and supply. If a locality shows signs of great residential development, it could be a smart choice to make an investment as the demands get triggered, which makes the prices grow. Even if people opt for renting instead of buying, it is also a good sign as renters convert into potential buyers.

Future Hotspots

Australian offices:

Australia is one of those developed countries which have maintained an impeccable record when it comes to growth and development. This record of Australia looks future proof because of the employment opportunities and population, which contribute to creating great investment opportunities in the future.

Co-working in Hong Kong:

Many of the landlords who deal in office spaces in Hong Kong have successfully managed to transform office spaces into some of the best event places, retail areas, and co-working office spaces.

Long-leased assets in the UK:

The real estate market of the UK offers diverse options for investors. One of the options the investors are leveraging is the option of long leased real estate. The long leased real estate investment option helps the investors approach the market differently. In the past few years, this sector has not only provided great investment options in industrial markets but also has rendered great opportunities for in non-core assets.

German retail:

Even though the retail sector is not always the first choice of investors, but the rise in population in Germany paired with consistent economic growth, is promising good growth in the coming years. Just because of these reasons, the market of European Logistics has seen undefined strengths since the year 2010. The lucrative market provides not only great opportunities for long-leased real estate but also provides amazing opportunities with strong agreements.

Portugal:

The prices of property in Rome and Barcelona are now equal to the prices of property in Lisbon's hot spots. So if you are looking to invest in the areas, the best bet would be to invest in the renovation projects. The same is true for Algarve. But even though the prices are on the rise, the rental rates have stayed unaffected. Even though the rent stays the same, the returns on the property would have been much higher if they were bought three years prior.

The market of Portugal also attracts more tourists every year and has also become one of the most famous destinations for foreign retirees. Though this fact upsets some Portuguese as this has impacted the price greatly, overall Portugal has emerged as a country with a strong and steady economy. The coast of Portugal as compared to Spain's coast is not overbuilt, all thanks to the serious and consequential restrictions imposed by the government on the further development of the oceanfront. Today, every new construction is restricted near the coast.

Panama:

Panama didn't suffer the crash in the year 2008/2009 as dramatically as other countries. One of the reasons being, Panama has a demand base broader than other countries. The prices in Panama City have increased multi-fold relative to the prices a decade-and-a-half ago. However, vis-à-vis global market, they tend to be a good buy on a per-square-meter basis and are promising enough to produce a robust and dependable rental return.

Netherlands:

Owing to its strong occupier market, this is in the top-list of many investors. The competition at Amsterdam is at the peak; however, there are several growth prospects in the neighboring Dutch cities like The Hague and Rotterdam. These two cities are also enjoying the knock-on effects of sturdy economic conditions, while the price levels are not as sharp as of Amsterdam, thereby giving private investors lucrative prospect to lock higher-yielding properties.

Europe:

Owing to the favorable blend of investment market momentum and sturdy fundamentals, the European market, especially the logistics market, has become robust and successful since the year 2010. It has become tough for private investors to acquire premium properties at profitable prices. One possible reason may be because mainland Europe has fascinated many institutional investors. Hence, for private investors, the alternative investment strategy can be to acquire higher-yielding secondary assets in urban areas or other good locations, the ones that have good residual land values. Later, in long-run, the assets can be transformed into logistics facilities.

USA:

Owing to the strength and multitude of the commercial real estate market of US the private investors require being innovative to dodge the competition with the investment trust market. The investors, who are in hunt of acquiring higher-yielding investments, can acquire assets in suburban areas, thereby benefitting from strong economic growth.

Brazil:

The country is anticipated to have around 18% rental returns for the townhouse. Having a weak currency against USD, Brazil is a lucrative option for dollar buyers. Particularly, Fortaleza can be given emphasis. It is likely to be an upcoming international tourist destination; however, it is considerably undervalued.

The only issue with Brazil is lack of accessibility. Brazil is a large country; hence, connecting flights make the travel time-consuming and tedious. However, several new direct flights that are introduced have made the Fortaleza airport much more accessible from Europe and North America. Consequently, the place is getting attention from foreign tourists.

9 PROFIT ANALYSIS FROM A DEAL IN REAL ESTATE

T o create a noticeable income from the real estate market, you can apply eight basic strategies. Your strategy decides what type of income you are going to earn, whether passive or active. These recommended strategies are:

1. Long-term residential rentals

Rentals from Buy-and-hold residential properties are one of the most applied methods for generating income from real estates. The rental properties will be evergreen, as the need of a residing place is always going to persist in the market. You need to carefully assess the amount for your property by ensuring three principles to follow, that are: location, location, and location.

The real estate majorly depends upon location. The location would not only increase the value of your property in the period but will also assist you in finding a tenant with long term staying objective. Choosing the best location for residential rental properties would bring higher advantages. The location should be set above the present status of the property. You can make perfect rental investments in run-down homes located in favorable locations.

This approach will involve traditional outlook for generating income through real estate market. This approach asks you to buy the property at a down payment and then keep it with you for a long duration. You can acquire a property with at least down payments or also for no down payments based on your status. If the property is already generating income or exists from quite a long time, then the situation becomes true.

You can make the best investment decision if your residential rental property has a positive flow of cash. You will find any such thing only if the owner of such residential property has to liquidate the property on an obligatory basis.

2. Lease options

To acquire an excellent credit at the outset or by without putting a substantial amount into the real estate market, you can get into the income generation of real estate by lease options. With a perspective of buying an option, you are leasing. If the real estate market stays on a growth rate, such things will work efficiently. It is because your purchase which will happen in the future depends on the price you are fixing in the current situation.

For instance, you must buy a property at a discounted rate when the prices are hiking. Even these rights of purchase can be effectively sold to another person by turning them around. This strategy depends on the bullish behavior of the real estate market. This option could be practiced as far as no one binds you to purchase the property at the end. And, this could turn the tables of profit for you.

3. Home-renovation flips

There has been a great increase in the fix-and-flip culture. The credit for unexpected growth in the renovation market has to go to increasing TRP of interior decoration shows on television. Going through this idea could be tricky but also assures great success. The lacking experience would let you to the downfall of this idea as you might fail to select the correct property.

4. Contract flipping

Flipping the contracts would be the easiest way without applying a lot of money or credit to the real estate market. In this approach, you need to introduce a desperate seller to a motivated buyer and see for the accomplishment of trade.

5. Short sales

When the property has not entered into the foreclosure, and the present owner of the property is under the mortgage, at this time short sales take place. This type of approach takes place when both the parties agree to this transaction based on the low prices of the property as the property is already mortgaged. You can make quick gains that too exempting the long-term renovations.

Getting benefits through short sales or any usual auctions practices can be sometimes tricky. You even don't get to see the site and are forced to pay in cash. In comparison to auctions, the short sales are a better choice they allow you to have a look at the property, which initiates the process of further negotiation. You must have a precise inspection and review of the property before getting into the purchase decision.

These sales are highly worthy, though it takes some time. You can earn a substantial return through a short sale. You can get a handsome amount as soon as you purchase the property. It is because the bank has stuck into a non-profitable investment. Though you must not assume that the property will be given at a very low price, you are still required to negotiate for a comparatively better price. The situation and the outcome depend on the urgency of the bank, as does it compromise with the given price or will wait for some other buyer.

6. Vacation Rentals:

The real estate market can increase profits through vacation rentals. If your property is located in a great tourist destination, then you can build a great amount of money through it. Such short-term rentals are highly popular in places like Los Angeles and Miami, including some great options.

7. Hard Money Lending:

The people, who legally don't pass the eligibility criteria of loans, are supported by these hard money lenders. Having a capital to back you up is required for hard money lending. Being given for brief periods, these loans have high rates of interests. Turning into a hard money lender would help close out the first deal. Your best foot forward could be having a "sure things" but lacking the capital. Hard money lending will not be your first venture into the real estate market, though you can earn great returns from it by making a great network of contacts, a great record of deals, and great capital.

Though, until you have a great amount of capital, you are allowed to select perfect deals that would allow small investment and can help you gain good returns. You can look for such investors who have grown into this sector easily. The rate of interest put is sensible. The reward and risk are both high. You would not require delaying the returns; instead, you can make short term investments and get good returns.

8. Commercial real estate

Investing in commercial properties is one of the most lucrative deals for real estate investors. In addition to the flipping, the developers also pay emphasis on developing these assets so that property has some added value, and the net gain is enhanced. Irrespective of the nature of the business, be it product-based or service-based, people require a place and space to run their offices and businesses, so it is mostly in demand. You can start investing in small or large spaces as per your budget and liquidity; however, as you grow, you can end up developing shopping malls and buildings.

10 CONCLUSION

Many people dream of being able to live on their rental income, but they shy away from the training and experience that they have to go through to reach that goal. Similarly, most people want results but aren't willing to put in the hard work that is required to achieve their goals. By writing this book, the author did his best to present the readers his personal experience in building up assets through real estate.

It is not about the money that makes you wealthy in the end; it is about the knowledge that you have acquired in the real estate business, as this enables you to learn from your mistakes and to start over and over again. As one wise man once said, "Success is based on the knowledge that can be easily implemented in practice."

ABOUT THE AUTHOR

Following a family tradition, Oswald Townsend discovered his passion for great architecture and landscape design during his teenage years. After the early stages of his career as an architect, he decided to solely specialize himself in real estate markets with a focus on Europe, North America, and Southeast Asia. As a means of sharing his founded experience, Townsend recently started writing books about the Real Estate business. Although traveling extensively, the center of his life is in London.

www.ingramcontent.com/pod-product-compliance
Lightning Source LLC
Chambersburg PA
CBHW070839220526
45466CB00002B/829